Supper

Supper

Reflections From Our Table

KARA A. KENNEDY

Supper: Reflections From Our Table

Copyright © 2020 by Kara Alexie Kennedy

All rights reserved. No part of this publication may be reproduced, stored in a retrieval system, or transmitted in any form by any means, electronic, mechanical, photocopy, recording, or otherwise, without the prior permission of the author except as provided for by USA copyright law.

Unless otherwise noted, all Scripture quotations are taken from the Holman Christian Standard Bible®, Used by Permission HCSB ©1999,2000,2002,2003,2009 Holman Bible Publishers. Holman Christian Standard Bible®, Holman CSB®, and HCSB® are federally registered trademarks of Holman Bible Publishers.

Scripture quotations marked AMP are taken from the Amplified Bible, Copyright © 1954, 1958, 1962, 1964, 1965, 1987 by The Lockman Foundation. Used by permission.

Scripture quotations marked CSB are been taken from the Christian Standard Bible®, Copyright © 2017 by Holman Bible Publishers. Used by permission. Christian Standard Bible•, and CSB® are federally registered trademarks of Holman Bible Publishers.

Scripture quotations marked GNT are from the Good News Translation in Today's English Version- Second Edition Copyright © 1992 by American Bible Society. Used by Permission.

Scripture taken from the International Children's Bible®. Copyright © 1986, 1988, 1999 by Thomas Nelson. Used by permission. All rights reserved.

Scripture quotations marked NIV are taken from the Holy Bible, New International Version®, NIV®. Copyright © 1973, 1978, 1984, 2011 by Biblica, Inc.® Used by permission of Zondervan. All rights reserved worldwide. www.zondervan.com The "NIV" and "New International Version" are trademarks registered in the United States Patent and Trademark Office by Biblica, Inc.®

Scripture quotations marked NLT are taken from the Holy Bible, New Living Translation, copyright ©1996, 2004, 2015 by Tyndale House Foundation. Used by permission of Tyndale House Publishers, a Division of Tyndale House Ministries, Carol Stream, Illinois 60188. All rights reserved.

Scripture quotations marked TLV Scripture taken from the Holy Scriptures, Tree of Life Version. Copyright © 2014,2016 by the Tree of Life Bible Society. Used by permission of the Tree of Life Bible Society.

Edited by Juan Carlos, Isabelle, and Julieana Osorio

First printing, 2020

Printed in the United States of America

ISBN: 978-1-7361275-0-6

For Granny
A warrior clothed in graceful quiet,
Whose refrain is an ever-open invitation
to come to the table
and eat

Reflections

Preface 11
A Winter Garden 15
Dirty Hands 23
Come and Eat 31
An Indian Thanksgiving 41
Crackers and Juice 49
Taboo 61
Dancing at the Dinner Table 73
Grief 81
When Jesus Wasn't Hungry 91
The Truth About Christians 97
Through Sugarcane and Tobacco 107
An Afternoon Walk 119
Wedding Invitations 129
Happy Hunting Grounds 135
Signposts 143
In Gratitude 149

Supper

Preface

The reflections in this book take their shape from memories and prayers that I share with my family. They form an invitation Home. Some stories have risen sheepishly from the pages of my private journals while others have jumped up like soapbox manifestos. Though they convene to form a deeply personal revelation of my identity, which was inherited and is daily rediscovered, each holds the prayer that I would not be seen, but Jesus.

To this end I have intentionally left blank space, in the details of the stories and in the pages themselves, hoping to get myself out of the way. This space represents the respite of silence that all image-bearers need: space to think, freedom to speak, stillness to listen.

I pray that the Holy Spirit would imbue these simple reflections with special significance, that they would be used by Jesus to form a personal, redemptive, irresistible invitation to dine at His table.

SUPPER

So neither he who plants nor he who waters is anything, but only God who gives the growth.

1 Corinthians 3:7

Supper

A Winter Garden

A heart attack stole into Christmas Eve. He was gone by New Year's Day.

The house was quick to fill with quintessential casseroles and flowers as we greeted the new year with grief. There was a moment that long winter day – purportedly short, but grief has a way of making the sun drag only stubbornly across the sky – in which I escaped to his garden for a breath of air. Perhaps it was a desperate attempt to find him there.

Two perfect rows of giant-leaved mustard greens defied the wintry chill and branched out proudly, their peppery spice my only clue as to what they were. Next to them hundreds of turnips peeked through tangled leaves like bright pink jewels studding the near-frozen ground.

Kennedy

I marveled.

I stared.

I wondered what on earth we would do.

The garden's abundance was almost humorous. Surely knowing he had left this massive harvest on our hands would have made Papa laugh out loud: no one particularly cared for mustard greens and turnips except for *him*. He would have found this quite funny.

But the memory of his good humor was cut short by the weight of silence.

On a normal winter's day in Arkansas, I would have relished this silence as a welcomed peace. The silence would have signaled that we had arrived at our much-anticipated respite from the noise of life back in Florida, a sure indicator that we were indeed home for the holidays, and a profound proof that the African proverb is true: *The road home is never too dark or too long.* On a normal winter's day in Arkansas, I would have simply closed my eyes and thanked God that I was there to be still and enjoy the silence.

But this was not a normal winter's day. This was the day without Papa. And the silence sucked any solace from the air,

Supper

leaving only a void. The garden, though full of life, was empty and alone.

I closed my eyes and tried to cover up the silence. I tried to imagine he was only in the garage, about to come out and wipe grease from his dirty hands onto even dirtier pants and ask me what I thought about his latest crop. I tried to imagine he was just around the corner fixing something, and that any moment he'd come back to tell me the story about where he got those mustard seeds from and why he'd forgotten to plant my kale. I tried to imagine that next summer I'd be back, and the garden would be even bigger, full of all the colors and flavors that he alone could coax up from that hard ground. I tried to imagine the day hadn't happened the way it did or brought the permanence that it did.

But when I opened my eyes, it was still silent, and he wasn't there.

It was just me and the turnips and the mustard greens.

I challenged the mustard.

Do you not know? Don't you realize? Papa's gone. He planted you but he's gone. He can't tend to you anymore. He'll never get to taste your leaves. Why do you keep on growing green as if he's still here? Why do you act like nothing's happened?

The mustard didn't answer.

In that irrational moment, just on the cusp of despair, I caught sight of an epiphany. It arrived as an act of mercy from the heavens: fresh words seemed to jump from the spicy leaves springing up from the ground and a new sound could almost be heard rustling among the turnips. Insight sprang forth and displaced the silence with wonder.

Yes, Papa was gone. But his garden continued to grow as if he never left. *His work had outlived him.*

A dear brother named Ravi used to wisely say, "The Lord buries His workers, but the Lord's work goes on."

I saw this truth made manifest in the garden leaves. Papa had died but the Lord's work – all He intended to bring about through Papa's life, hands, and legacy which would proclaim His truth and bring Him glory – would go on growing. The mustard greens were living proof. And we, gathered there in his home grieving him amid casseroles and flowers, were living proof, too.

It is a delightful fate that Papa's last garden boasted the promise of mustard seeds.

The humble mustard seed had inspired Jesus more than once. Eyeing it, He claimed that faith even that small could command the desert-loving mulberry tree to be uprooted and planted in hostile, salty seas.[1] He believed faith that small could summon the audacity to command mountains.[2] He saw in the mustard seed the Kingdom of God made manifest on earth, appearing at first small but full of hidden promise, and capable of growing into a life-giving shelter for others.[3]

Was Papa thinking of these things when he planted them? Likely not. But grace can steep the everyday works of our lives with supernatural significance whether we recognize it or not.

Thousands of years after Jesus had stood in the Judean countryside marveling at the Father's glory revealed in seeds, I stood in Papa's last garden marveling at where the seeds could point us: to the unseen Kingdom of God.

Even after his death, the fruits of Papa's labors would continue to flourish, expand, manifest, multiply. *Such is the way of the Kingdom, to refuse to be stopped by the grave.*

The seasons have since turned but Papa's garden continues to point us to the Kingdom. I couldn't resist taking a picture at that moment when the garden leaves began to rustle with this truth and hope. I am determined not to let that long winter day

---

[1] Luke 17:5-6
[2] Matthew 17:20
[3] Luke 13:18-19

end. It is frozen in canvas in our dining room. Every sojourner the Lord brings to our table inevitably takes notice of the curious winter garden hanging prominently in our sunny Florida home. They ask for the story. And truth and hope jump from the leaves afresh, boldly proclaiming again what they spoke that day: that any work of the Lord in our lives has the capacity to outlive us.

These enduring works serve to point others onward to the place where sleeping workers wake, to that unseen Kingdom where Papa and Ravi alike will someday be glad to greet us.

SUPPER

Now I call you friends.

John 15:15 ICB

Supper

Dirty Hands

My grandmother birthed five children, who collectively had ten children, who have so far given life to nine more children and counting. She has not moved from her rural Arkansas home in over fifty years, making her the victim of three full generations of mud-pie-making misadventures in her lawn.

In the very same yard that once hosted the make-believe exploits of our parents, my cousins and I used to indulge the dog days of summer inventing muddy fun together. Today, our children are the third generation to delight in that same humble dirt which curious little hands can't seem to resist digging up under Granny's otherwise green grass.

This continuity and simplicity in our upbringing, epitomized by our playtime, might naïvely suggest we would all continue lockstep with one another as we grew up. The reality, of course, is that our paths have taken us wildly different places, as paths of life always do. All of us have strayed from the simple ethics and Christian values that constituted our moral upbringing. All of us have rebelled to one extent or another. All of us have chosen paths that are different from the path our parents or Granny or our childhood selves would have chosen for us. All of us have dirty hands of one sort or another.

In spite of our wanderings, Granny remains the centripetal force that pulls all of us together. Her house is the one place in the world where it is impossible to arrive too early or stay too late. Granny always wishes we would have arrived sooner, and always invites us to stay longer. Despite our rebellions and shortfalls, hers is a house of eternal welcome.

Surely, she is not naïve. She knows our rebellious ways more than we might care to admit. Yet she most often chooses to remain silent about those matters as we sit at her table and eat (no doubt saving all her words for Jesus, to whom she tirelessly intercedes on our behalf). Rather than lecture or correct us, she prefers to simply enjoy our presence at the table, even if it means our hands are still dirty from whatever mess we've gotten ourselves into in the outside world. She's no stranger to kids going outside and playing in the mud anyway.

And neither is Jesus. He, too, offers an open-ended invitation to His dirty-handed children to come inside and eat, expressed most beautifully through first communion.

COMMUNION

The first communion is situated in a startling context of death, betrayal, fighting, and failure. There's an awful lot of filth to tinge the unfolding drama.

Outside, the religious elite are plotting to kill Jesus.[1] His heart for the outcast and His radical departure from their privileged ways are too much for them.

They elicit the help of an insider, Judas. His loyalty is bought for a pittance and he readily plots to betray Jesus.[2] Tension mounts as the hour draws near.

Meanwhile, Jesus has gathered His disciples for the Passover feast. Despite the solemnness of the occasion, the disciples erupt in a juvenile quarrel at the table over which of them is the greatest.[3] They seem oblivious to the holiness and

---

[1] Matthew 26:4
[2] Matthew 26:14-16
[3] Luke 22:24

humility that epitomizes their leader. They cannot see this Selfless Servant in their midst – they cannot see past themselves.

But their selfish quarrels and Judas' selfish scheming are not all that plague the evening. After this meal is finished, Jesus will face the darkest hour of His eternal existence and the *only* thing He will ask of His disciples, His closest friends, is that they stay awake and pray for Him. But they will fail Him, falling asleep multiple times even when Jesus confesses He is sorrowful to the point of death and begs them to stay awake and pray.[1]

When the enemy does come for Jesus, the disciples will falter yet again, running away in fear. They will leave Jesus to face His trial completely alone.[2]

Despite his self-proclaimed fervency for Christ, Peter will deny three times that he even knows Jesus.[3]

Right in the center of all these downfalls and travesties, as if situated in the still eye of a raging hurricane of controversy, a table is set and the very first communion is served.

---

[1] Matthew 26:36-46
[2] Matthew 26:56
[3] Mark 14:30

SUPPER

As He prepares for this special meal, Jesus knows His disciples have and will fail Him. He knows they will betray Him; they won't be there when He most needs them. Even though He taught them well, He knows they'll fight at the table. They come to dinner with dirty hands. And yet, knowing all of this, He looks at these weak, broken, sinful, scared men, and calls them *friends*. He says He wants to be remembered by them. He humbles Himself beneath them, and serves them bread and wine, and offers them the Kingdom of God.

This is extravagant grace.

COME AND EAT

The invitation to His disciples continues today. In the same way that Granny has always made room for us at her table, even if our hands are filthy and our ways are wrong, so Jesus makes room for us at His.

When we approach His table, He knows how we've failed Him in the past, how we are selfish and rebel against Him today, how we will betray Him tomorrow. He knows that too often we can't even bring ourselves to get along with the other people He's invited to the table with us. He knows who we are and how we behave. Our hands are dirty from following the ways of the world and the ways of our hearts. And *knowing us* – knowing what we've done against Him and how we'll fail

Him next – He calls us friends. He says, *"Come, feast. I give you bread and wine that satisfy. A feast that will remind you that the best is yet to come."*

Do you believe this?

Each of us has taken roads we shouldn't have. Each of us has dirty hands. Each of us knows we are undeserving to dine at such a wonderful table as Christ's. And yet, the truth is, that He has reserved a seat for us. His love for us is such that He delights in our presence at the table.

His house is like Granny's. It's impossible to arrive too early or stay too late. He always wishes we had arrived sooner, and always invites us to stay longer. Despite our rebellions and shortfalls, His is a house of eternal welcome.

SUPPER

and behold, an angel touched him and said to him, "Get up and eat."

1 kings 19:5 AMP

SUPPER

Come and Eat

Granny never seems to tire of the classic Southern overture to every meal: "Come and eat!"

During the summer of 2020, my daughters and I took her up on the invitation. It took almost fifteen hours to get to her table, and we arrived mentally and physically exhausted, toting along with us no shortage of the problems and worries that had globally plagued the year.

The table she set was one of great love. She had whipped nostalgia into her mashed potatoes and coated locally grown squash and okra with Southern cornmeal sweetened with sugar; she had baked a special loaf of bread that was a gift from my mother and prepared a dish that holds immeasurable value to my sentimental palate: some of the last peas saved from my grandfather's last summer garden.

Arriving to Granny's house feels like entering the world of Middle-earth penned in pages long ago. In the fantasy classic *The Lord of the Rings,* Tolkien described the blessings and relief that fell upon his humble hobbit named Frodo as he at last maneuvered dangers and made it to the relative safety of the elven valley called Rivendell. Frodo had passed through many troubles, and his enemies were still hot on his heals. They sought him with a fury, plotting many evils in the long and arduous road sprawling before him. But for the moment, partway between his home and his destination, between the dangers of yesterday and the dangers of tomorrow, the little hobbit was able to pause in Rivendell:

> *"Frodo was now safe in the Last Homely House east of the Sea. That house was…'a perfect house, whether you like food or sleep or story-telling or singing, or just sitting and thinking best, or a pleasant mixture of them all.' Merely to be there was a cure for weariness, fear, and sadness."*

To arrive to Granny's house, especially in the turmoil and upset of 2020, is to arrive to Rivendell.

Supper

When I collapsed into a chair to finally eat, the havoc that had riddled our journey and our everyday disposition was suddenly quieted by the unassuming power of this homecooked meal. The chaos and uncertainty swirling outside felt almost irrelevant while dining in the security of Granny's table. From what felt like a safe distance, I pondered the problems and worries that were – at least temporarily – silenced:

We live in a time of war, division, and violence that is exacerbated by an unprecedented measure of socialized censorship and eager abandonment of truth. These external forces intensify the internal wars that wage within us, as worries about health, finances, and security impede upon our thought life and disrupt our peace. Truly, these times are so dark that the weeks following 9/11, the saddest historical season of my lifetime, can now be reminisced as the 'good ole days' in comparison to the present.

If Granny's table had been set in the serene bliss of a utopian world, it would have been lost in the plenty of many other wonderful meals. But because the table was set in a backdrop of ongoing war, in the presence of real enemies, the meal stood out as a rare and precious goodness, something to be treasured and revered. In some sense, the darkness outside actually did more to sweeten the meal than Granny's sweet tea because it provided the contrast to make her table appear that much brighter.

Taking one last bite before getting up to indulge in seconds, I mused at the way this dinner left me oddly, scandalously grateful for my enemies and freshly aware of Jesus.

Believers and skeptics alike ask what Jesus is doing amid the darkness, violence, and chaos that characterizes our cultural moment. Behind this question lurks the spoken or silent challenge that He is not doing anything, or not doing enough. But I believe He is doing something quite a lot like my Granny: quietly preparing a table for us.[1]

Much like the elves in Tolkien's Rivendell, He has an admirable penchant for hospitality in the middle of war.

Psalm 23

Psalm 23 is arguably the most famous psalm ever penned. "Yea, though I walk through the valley of the shadow of death..." are the words wielded by priests against evil spirits in horror films, recited in predictably rainy grave-side funeral scenes, and iconified 1990's-style in the opening lines of "Gangsta's Paradise." Number 23 is consistently the most searched for Psalm on the internet and is made subject to

---

[1] Psalm 23:4 KJV

endless allegorical interpretations. It has been appropriated by artists and theologians and heretics alike to become a cultural icon. But let's not allow its familiarity to dull its wonder.

Psalm 23 evokes the wartime hospitality of Jesus.

In the Presence of My Enemies

Note that He prepares a table for us *in the presence* of our enemies. He doesn't care that our enemies are still present among us, taunting us and laying claim to a spiritual landscape that's really His. He doesn't care that battles are still raging, and smoke is still smoldering from the destructive fires the enemy has set to our comforts. He isn't intimidated by their jeering or their threats.

As the Victor of all victors, He establishes His presence right in the midst of their violence and invites us to pull up a chair to replenish.

Jesus doesn't wait for the darkness to leave or the war to end before inviting us to eat. He invites us in the middle of it all. He invites us while our enemies stand by and watch.

It is true, of course, that the enemy conspires to keep us from accepting His invitation and perhaps this explains why so many of us challenge Jesus' whereabouts in dark times. The enemy will distract us with busyness, worry, guilt, torment, and bitterness. The enemy will stir up quarrels with the other people who are invited to that table, fuel resentment toward Jesus for not doing enough to stop our pain, or engender personal shame that insists we are undeserving of the invitation. Just as the Black Riders relentlessly pursued Frodo up to the very moment he passed through the gates of Rivendell, so the enemy will pursue us with any lie or scheme or distraction in the hopes that we might not make it to Jesus' table.

But it is also true that Jesus never tires of making the invitation, and His active offer to dine at His table endures, *and shines brightest*, in the presence of darkness.

I WILL FEAR NO EVIL

Sitting at Granny's table, I was overcome with gratitude, not *in spite* of my enemies, but *because* of them.

I wasn't grateful in spite of the pandemic, but because of the pandemic.

I wasn't grateful in spite of global upset, but because of global upset.

I wasn't grateful in spite of so many challenges at work, but because of so many challenges at work.

Supper

All the forces of darkness I could perceive around us became channels of gratitude because they helped me enjoy the blessings at this special table all the more.

Such is the ultimate sovereignty and goodness of Christ in our darkest valleys: sitting at the table He prepares for us transforms our fear of the surrounding darkness into a *scandalously bold gratitude*. The darkness provides the necessary contrast to help us see how bright and rare His goodness really is. In this way, the darkness fuels our love for Jesus.

The implications of this truth are profound. It means I can thank God for the dark valleys and the cheating cleverness of our enemies. I can thank Him for the pains of labor and the onslaught of daily challenges. I can thank God for the brokenness, division, plagues, and the many barriers erected against any hope of earthly paradise. I can thank God when there is war and not peace. I can thank Him *for* these things, not despite them. And where there is so much gratitude, *so much love*, there is no room for fear.[1]

Admittedly, the dark times we suffer hold a very real power. But the Scriptures collectively insist that theirs is not a power to be feared. Darkness only holds the power which Christ

---

[1] 1 John 4:18

Himself bestows upon it. We already know that He grants the darkness power to contrast with light, helping us appreciate the good. He also grants darkness the power to refine us in the same way that fire refines gold, making us more like Christ.[1] And He grants darkness the power to dispel any idea we might hold that earth is Home. Instead, the impending darkness serves to remind us that we should not settle too comfortably here but remember that all whom Christ has redeemed are citizens of Heaven.[2] We are sojourners merely passing through the Temporary Seen on our way to the Eternal Unseen.[3]

This collective power that Jesus gives to darkness can be seen in the proper light only as we dine at His table with the darkness in view – in the presence of our enemies.

For this and so many reasons, we should fear no evil. God promises to use it for our good.[4]

For You are with Me

Ultimately, Jesus proves Himself to be one of purpose and provision during war. He gives purpose to the darkness that

---

[1] 1 Peter 1:7
[2] Philippians 3:20
[3] 2 Corinthians 4:18
[4] Romans 8:28

Supper

schemes against us while providing supernatural provision to refresh and sustain us at His table. He offers the respite and richness of Rivendell and the sweetness and security of Granny's Southern table. He wields His sovereignty over absolutely everything for His glory and our good.

And He does it all with His standing wartime invitation to *come and eat.*

For Viviana and Kenton, who taught me what
Jesus does in the presence of our enemies.

Now go home and have a feast. Share your food and wine with those who don't have enough. Today is holy to our Lord, so don't be sad.

Nehemiah 8:10 GNT

SUPPER

An Indian Thanksgiving

Turkey
Ham
Cornbread dressing
Green bean casserole
Sweet potato casserole
Corn casserole
White beans
Mashed potatoes
Cranberry sauce
Buttered rolls
Cheese ball
Pecan, pumpkin, and coconut pies
Cherry cheesecake
And anything else the women are inspired to prepare

The Thanksgiving spread at Granny's house could be rivaled in richness only by the unbounded laughter that reverberated off the walls. There was never a moment of silence but an endless stream of stories and jokes thanks to the sheer number of relatives able to squeeze into such a compact space.

But one pivotal year tore our family of five away from those treasured traditions. A burgundy minivan, as light with hope as it was weighed with luggage, pulled out of the pebble driveway where we used to ride our bikes and set off toward Florida sunsets and new beginnings.

The novelty of our new adventures in the sun wore off as soon as the leaves back home began to change. Florida leaves had the peculiar ability to stay green. It got colder in Arkansas. It stayed hot in Florida.

And a stark and sweaty Thanksgiving Day commanded we take stock of reality: For the first time, our relatives were gathering around Granny's table, but we were one thousand miles too far away to join them.

Perhaps this hit no one harder than my mom, who alone was burdened to cook, craft, create, and curate all the casseroles and pies we associated with our traditional turkey feast. I was eight years old, and I can remember my exhausted mother paying the long-distance phone charges to call her mom to

Supper

lament, while never ceasing her work in the kitchen, crying and overwhelmed that she was knee-deep in the daunting task of Thanksgiving all alone. It was a labor of days that would be eaten, not amidst the ambience of incessant laughter and joyous greetings to which we were accustomed, but in the awkward silence of a remnant torn away and out of place, longing for home.

Twenty-seven Thanksgivings later, we still feast a thousand miles away, and we continue to carry that longing for home, though the passage of time has softened its sting. My mom labors for days creating a nostalgic feast for the senses, always adding a new experimental dish or two among the all-star tried-and-trues. Our house could never be as full as Granny's and the laughter could never ring quite so loud, but my mom has made it her mission to fill this void by inviting people as displaced as we once were to partake in our family traditions. Even though our guests aren't privy to the experience around Granny's table which our distant Thanksgivings strive to simulate, many find themselves drawn year over year to return to the table my mom has created.

All of this has opened my eyes to a world that naivety otherwise would have concealed.

Recently, our new neighbors invited my husband and me over for a "casual gathering with snacks." The faint scent of curry met us at the front door and led the way to a kitchen table spread with an exotic feast of kings. (Clearly, I had misunderstood that "snacks" was a polite understatement.)

I sensed at once that we had entered a decadent world of color and flavor and complex divinities completely unique and *other*. Tandoori chicken and marinated paneer cheese were accompanied by tiny samosas, edamame spring rolls, mint sauce and sticky-sweet chutneys. Curries and spices were chased with cooling cucumber and mango salad. Honeycomb laced an assortment of cheeses and artfully arranged nuts and fruits on large wooden trays. Pistachio and mango cheesecake – made with yogurt instead of cheese – boasted purposefully placed blueberries that adorned every slice. My eyes lit up as I found myself enveloped in the famed Indian hospitality that I had previously only read about in books. My only regret was that I had eaten dinner before coming over.

Our conversation lingered long into the night, punctuated with generous offers for more food and drink. Our gregarious hosts saw to our every need while enriching our conversation with questions and jokes. With our hearts as full as our stomachs, we made our way to their front door.

Supper

Our final exchange turned to traditional religious and holiday feasts, which my new friend is tasked with cooking every year. Struggling to take queues from my embarrassingly limited knowledge of Hindu culture, I asked if they celebrate their feasts with large family gatherings. This rather benign question turned their spirits, and their eyes spoke what words did not.

Their eyes, which have beheld a land so unfamiliar to my own, which fixate on gods so inapposite to my One, which read languages so foreign to mine and perceive the world through a view so different to mine, were suddenly as familiar as Granny's cornbread dressing. They revealed the same words I had read in my mom's eyes twenty-seven Thanksgivings ago: a longing for family around the festive table.

Stumbling to fill the silence with politeness and restraint, I asked a dumb and obvious question which I regretted as soon as I voiced it:

"Don't you have any family living nearby?"

Of course not, stupid. That's why there's so few at their holiday feasts.

But they surprised me with a gracious a smile. Their eyes lit up.

"Yes, absolutely, of course we do! We have family living just right over there."

To my amazement, raising a hand to gesture, our new friend pointed across the street to our home.

Sharing feasts and stories has a way of fostering unexpected families and bridging unlikely worlds.

Later that night, I considered how I wouldn't have fully appreciated the meticulously flavored traditional Indian dishes or recognize the pain I saw in their eyes if the foundation for feasting and storytelling had not been laid all those Thanksgivings past, where tradition wrote the menu and drew the near and far together.

But the question remains: how? How could peoples and traditions so foreign echo a longing so familiar?

When my daughters were much younger, they had an annoying habit of answering all my deep questions with the unsure and lazy guess, "God?"

They automatically assumed that the response to every life question I asked was "God" and sometimes mixed it up a bit by guessing "Jesus." Even though I frequently challenged them about this assumption, to be fair, they were usually right.

Supper

This universal longing to gather with family to feast and celebrate is planted within all of us by God, who has placed "eternity in our hearts"[1] and given us a longing for our real Home. It does not matter whether we recognize Him or not. We can worship other gods or idols, develop a worldview incongruous to the Scriptures, and shroud ourselves in worldly or spiritual colors, but we cannot remove the universal longing He has placed within us: that longing to gather as family in festive celebration at His table.

In this way, every table, no matter how near or far to God, is an echo of that universal longing for Home. Every feasting table is a signal, not merely to look back and seek to replicate the holiday of yesteryear, but to look forward toward the bounty and joy that Heaven's tables hold for us. This is what brings us together, no matter how far apart we might be.

---

[1] Ecclesiastes 3:11

He was made known to them in the breaking of the bread.

Luke 24:35

SUPPER

Crackers and Juice

A Saturday night at Granny's house would always lend itself to Sunday morning at Granny's church. This hour of worship – a child's eternity – always entailed the solemn passing of shiny metal plates, the contents of which seemed harmless enough but for reasons no child can appreciate, these particular plates of crackers and Welch's were strictly off limits. Holiness was still a lofty concept lingering very high above my childhood reach, but on Sundays in Batesville, Arkansas it would inevitably take on the humble form of unleavened bread and popular juice and pass – temptingly close – across my lap, out of my grasp, and on to the next adult.

Years later, a Saturday night at Granny's house still lends itself to Sunday morning at Granny's church, though an hour of worship now feels too short. When those shiny metal plates pass, the nostalgic bread and juice take on a heightened dimension of worship, and the child within me secretly relishes the triumph that the plates no longer pass over her head. Communion is now within reach. But what is it that renders Communion so sacred that it was kept out of reach for so long?

Unbeknownst to children who are merely eyeing a trivial snack, Holy Communion is so heavily weighted with spiritual force that mishandling it led to sickness and death in the early Church.[1] The feast holds no less power and authority today. Whether the bread and wine serve as a symbolic representation or miraculous transubstantiation is a theological query that must be relegated to the periphery, for another book and another moment. The current question – one whose answer can lead to a clearer appreciation for why that plate is so holy that it can and indeed *should* be passed over us at times:

What is it that's being passed?

Placing the original elements into their biblical context unearths treasures to behold.

---

[1] 1 Corinthians 11:29-30

Supper

"THIS IS MY BODY."

Bread enjoys a privileged role in the Scriptures, its significance spanning life, salvation, unity, forgiveness, the very Word of God, and Christ Himself.

Bread has served as a reminder to humanity of God's love, provision, and sustenance. It was carried in haste out of Egyptian slavery, rained down miraculously in exile, routinely baked throughout ages and cultures, and today is found warming the Southern kitchen. Christ was born in Bethlehem – the House of Bread – and made His divine nature known time and again in the breaking of the bread. He miraculously multiplied it in the countryside, He proved His mercy by sharing it with sinners, He chose to be remembered by it, and He revealed Himself after the resurrection by breaking it with His disciples.

So entrenched in spiritual meaning is bread that to enjoy even the humblest portion of it is to enjoy a shadow of Christ Himself.

Bread can teach us things.

The very making of bread basks in the shadow of God's own creative power. As Rabbi David Foreman has illuminated, the Hebrew word for dough, from which we make bread, also means clay, from which God made man. A closer look reveals the Gospel message has been written into the science of the making of bread: Wheat is harvested – killed – before its life-giving seeds are separated from the chaff and ground into flour. In this killing, breaking, and grinding, the wheat is stripped of life and left to wait. Then, in the act of baking bread, water is added back into the wheat and it awakens into new life. A series of chemical reactions transforms the flour and water into something entirely new: bread. This loaf, once wheat that gave its life over to death, is now fully alive and transformed into bread, to be the nourishment on which mankind subsists. Jesus – the ultimate Artist and Creator, who understood the intimate details of the creation of bread, called Himself the Bread of Life.[1]

In the act of Communion, bread is elevated to become a tangible experience of Truth, a conduit through which we might experience an intimate encounter with Christ as He chose to be remembered.

"THIS IS MY BLOOD."

The wine that rounds out His sacred supper is as steeped in spiritual significance as the bread. Wine in the Hebrew Bible represents joy for both God and man.[2] It is not merely joy for

---

[1] John 6:35
[2] Judges 9:13; Psalm 104:15

Supper

joy's sake, but rather the fullness of joy in the completed work of God.

This is expressed in the Levitical drink offering, which could be made only once God's people had entered the Promised Land and were in full possession of the blessing God had secured for them. The drink offering faithfully accompanied the burnt, meal, and peace offerings of ancient Israel, a ritualistic repetition that underscored God's ongoing joy in His completed work. This invitation to worship God and please Him based on His work and not our own efforts is the epitome of grace.

But the layers of meaning don't end there. Wine is a surprising mediator of biblical truth. The book of Joel tells the story of God disciplining a sinful and rebellious Israel with a plague of locusts. The insects devoured the fruit of the vine and destroyed any hope for a harvest. No harvest meant no wine, and no wine meant no drink offerings. Because the drink offering signifies God's joy and pleasure, removing the possibility of making a drink offering by allowing the grapes to be destroyed sent a clear message from the heavens that God was not pleased with their sinfulness.

"Grain and drink offerings have been cut off from the house of the Lord... mourn... Be ashamed... because the harvest of the field has perished. The grapevine is dried up...Indeed, human joy has dried up."[1]

And yet, as with so many biblical stories, this narrative is steeped in grace and ends in hope. Upon repentance, God blessed the harvest so that new wine could be made, restoring the opportunity to make a drink offering and sending a new message from the heavens, one that would find its echo centuries later in Jesus' parable of the prodigal son: that there is great joy in repentance.

Wine heralds divine grace, intimacy, spiritual transformation, and God's blessings. It urges us to repentance.

Jesus had a purposed affinity to this treasured fruit of the vine. He chose wine-making – the best wine at a wedding feast – as the first reported miracle of His earthly life. His famous teaching of the True Vine, in which He weaved together the purpose of life, joy and righteousness, the Communion of God and man, the nature of authentic relationship, the beauty of discipline, and the existence of the Trinity, ultimately points to the wine for which the vine's fruit is grown. Communion wine is the culmination of teachings about God's sacred work of cleansing and reconciling humanity unto Himself; it represents the new covenant. It can neither be overstated nor

---

[1] Joel 1:9-12

fully understood the full depth of wisdom which Christ wills to teach us through wine.

Drink this in. Wine is that storied elixir which carries divine poetry in its color, its fragrance, and its taste. It ever calls us back to the True Vine. This joy of God and man is carefully selected to be shared in the Communion feast. Jesus likens it to His own sacred blood, a defiant declaration signaling the finality of the ancient sacrificial system: with the shedding of His blood, the sacrifice would be complete. A new way, a new covenant, a new joy would cover His people.

"DO THIS IN REMEMBRANCE OF ME."

As Jesus prepared His disciples to carry His Name forward in the days following His death, He could have emulated common ways that many of history's notable figures have sought to preserve their legacies. The Buddha chose to be remembered through pilgrimage, asking his followers to retrace his steps from birth to enlightenment, that his path might inspire their own. George Washington wanted to be remembered as the leader of a republic and not a monarchy, President and not king, and ensured each successive president would remember the same by following his actions to step down from power. John Lennon purportedly worried to Paul McCartney about how he would be remembered by fans just before his untimely death. The way we wish to be remembered reveals a great deal about us.

As for Jesus, He had a lot of options. He was a brilliant teacher. His command over the Scriptures and keen understanding into the hidden ways of the heart left critics in stunned silence and followers in stunned awe. Today, He is known even among non-believers as one of the single greatest teachers of all time. Surely, He could have chosen to be remembered by the recitation of His teachings and parables.

He didn't.

He was an unmatched miracle-worker. His supernatural feats signaled the immanence of the Kingdom of God and offered glimpses into the fully restored and reconciled life that God alone has the power to bring about. These sightings of Heaven brought Him an unsolicited celebrity status that He consciously ran away from. But knowing the power of His work to prove His divinity and favor from the Father, He could have chosen to be remembered by the retelling of His miracles.

He didn't.

He was an itinerant preacher, having traveled the highways and byways, countryside and capital, deserts and seas in search of those who would listen, repent, and follow the One

SUPPER

who had no place to lay His head.[1] He walked thousands of miles bringing good news to the poor, healing the brokenhearted, proclaiming freedom to captives, and comforting those who mourn.[2] The places He visited were known to the ancient world and well-documented. He could have chosen to be remembered by a pilgrimage retracing of His steps.

He didn't.

Instead of requesting any retelling, reciting, or retracing, He did something entirely unexpected. He chose to be remembered in the sharing of bread and wine, a feast of friends.

He did not want fame. He wanted to be *known*. Known, not for what He said or did, but for who He was.

There is a story recorded in Luke which has ever-endeared me to Jesus. It was the third day after His crucifixion, and two of His followers were on the road to Emmaus. Jesus appeared to walk alongside them, but they didn't recognize Him. They updated this traveling stranger on the whirlwind events of the past three days, and Jesus responded in true rabbinical style. He thoughtfully connected the dots between what they had

---
[1] Luke 9:58
[2] Isaiah 61:1-3

witnessed and the prophetic Scriptures, a comprehensive theological discourse pointing all evidence to the Messiah (which I would give anything to have heard). But they still didn't recognize Him. Finally, they arrived at the place where they were staying and invited Jesus to join them for dinner. When He gave thanks and broke the bread, *then* they recognized Him! They knew Jesus not as a traveler or a rabbi, but as one who broke bread with them. One who came into their home and ate.[1]

This is the kind of God we worship: one who ate with us then, who eats with us now, and who will eat with us in glory.

Holiness is still far above my reach. But I have grown just a bit taller over the years and have caught at least a glimpse of what's really happening Sunday mornings at Granny's church. Communion is no mere sharing of crackers and juice. It is a supernatural moment in time when that fateful final supper is brought into the glorious view of a future wedding feast, held together in the unassuming present moment where we find ourselves quietly passing a plate.

---

[1] Luke 24:13-35

SUPPER

My kingdom is not of this world.

John 18:36

Supper

Taboo

My husband is proud to be an American. Born in Bogotá, he moved to the United States at the age of 18 to complete his undergraduate studies. Fast forward, and the Lord surprised him with a wife and two daughters. Now he's here to stay.

He went through the naturalization process during an election year and, with the promise of the right to vote just on the horizon, he took up a keen interest in politics. Having not grown up under the stars and stripes, he had a bias neither to the left or the right and quite innocently just wanted to learn more about the country he was hoping to call his own. What better way to learn about a country than to ask its citizens their opinions? To my horror, that's exactly what he did.

Many a lovely dinner with friends and professional colleagues were rendered awkward and tense as my curious husband unwittingly triggered guests with his political questions. No topic was taboo to him; he just wanted to learn about our penchants toward donkeys or elephants or tea. He relished the vast array of conflicting answers his inquiries produced in dinner after dinner.

Alas, he seemed not to know that curiosity can kill a cat. On more than one night, as these conversations wore on endlessly and guests clamored for the final word in a dinnertime debate, I sat there staring at the cold, forgotten coffee and uneaten desserts and silently mused how my husband was in danger of suffering the fate of the cat. He was just too curious.

Religion and Politics

The two taboo topics at most tables, especially during an election year, are religion and politics. To avoid these at a dinner party is to virtually guarantee a more delightful meal with guests.

Politics is arguably the more dangerous of the two taboos today. In our post-truth society, we can hide our religious persuasions behind the poorly constructed claim that you can have "your truth" and I can have "my truth" and the real "Truth" doesn't exist or matter, so all our religions can be deemed equal for purposes of polite conversation.[1]

Politics does not allay itself so easily. Even among Christians, who purportedly share a similar worldview and can (or should) freely speak of religion, politics is still commonly banned for its power to divide or trigger.

This, I believe, is because the ancient art of conversation is at the brink of extinction. We Americans seem no longer able to engage in civil disagreements. We are beginning to think with our emotions rather than our reason, discard absolutes in favor of relatives, and muddle our ideas with our person. In the past, one could disagree with a person's ideas but still value and respect the person. This is foundational to civil discourse. Today, because the person understands that his ideas make up who he *is*, to disagree with his ideas is equivalent to rejecting *him* as a person. Mix in our cultural fascination with victimhood and we have a perfect storm for

---

[1] This uniform embrace of 'everything as equal' ultimately strips time-honed faith systems of their sharp edges and multicolored distinctions in favor of the dull gray monotony of pluralism, where everything is considered fundamentally alike. But the dulling of the world that pluralism ironically proffers is for another essay and another time. I shall digress...

fruitless, defensive, ill-informed conversations in which everyone walks away a victim.

The tempting remedy is to silence political conversations. This will grant us a bit of peace at the dinner table. It will spare us from triggers and awkwardness. It will allow us to finish the night laughing and delighted with an evening void of any risky substance. But is this the type of artificial dinnertime peace we want?

W.W.J.D.

My daughters are currently sporting the renaissance of the "W.W.J.D." bracelets that decades ago adorned every Christian kid in my high school. The trend is back. The question the bracelet poses is timeless. *What Would Jesus Do?*

Jesus engaged in politics. He never cowered and He did not shut down disagreeable conversations. Ever ready to give an answer, or more often a cleverer question, Jesus freely engaged in the politics of His day. His brilliant and famous line, "Give to Caesar the things that are Caesar's and to God the things that are God's," was a response to a question about whether people should pay their taxes. It was also posed with the express intent of trying to trick Him into a political trap. Knowing all of this, Jesus rendered an ingenious response that not only answered the question but also silenced those plotting against Him.[1]

He also worked a surprising bit of humor into His opinions. The nuanced political commentary woven into the parable of the barren fig tree can be lost to modern readers. But here, Jesus implies in rather comic pundit fashion that some leaders (Pilate being the politician He had just mentioned) need a little manure smeared on them.[2]

Yes, God is hilarious.

Not only does Jesus model a healthy engagement in controversial political discussions *in particular*, but He also immortalizes both the cost and value of engaging in controversial discussions *in general*. Easily the most controversial statement ever made is that Jesus is God. He made no secret of this claim and His boldness cost His life (in the hands of political and religious leaders, no less).[3] His audacious adherence to this truth claim also produced untold eternal fruit and set all of Heaven into joyous celebration for the immeasurable good He accomplished which no mortal or angel can fully fathom.[4] We are assured that "for the joy set

---

[1] Matthew 22:15-22
[2] Luke 13:1-9
[3] Matthew 26:57-68
[4] 1 Peter 1:12

before Him, He endured the cross."[1] He was willing to count the cost of speaking up, and then pay it.

If Jesus refused to back down from difficult or risky conversations, neither can we. He is not our only example. Our Founding Fathers lived in a time of great political dreams and dangers. The opinions they held about life, liberty, and the pursuit of happiness were taboo to the point of death. They encountered disagreements, arguments, threats, financial losses, and surely many an "uncomfortable" dinner party. But they continued their conversations about politics, counting the cost of speaking up and willing to pay it. For their boldness and commitment to speaking truth, they birthed a nation.

Having inherited such a legacy of costly, fruitful discourse and knowing full well the generational blessings produced by bold convictions, dare we shy away from those conversations at the table that might cost us an evening?

EMINENT DOMAIN

Another objection posed among some of our Christian friends is that politics should simply be left to the side. The idea is that Christians should gather and talk about Jesus but should keep quiet about politics.

---

[1] Hebrews 12:2 TLV

Supper

God forbid we upset anyone.

Not only is this problematic because it ignores the active and engaged lifestyle that Jesus Himself modeled, but it assumes that politics is its own domain that can be separated out from the Christian experience. This line of thought unwittingly steals from Jesus.

Yes, "steal" is a strong word. It's the right word to use.

If Jesus is my Lord, He has claim over all of me. His is a sacred form of eminent domain. There is not a single thought that fleets across my mind that is not subject to His rule. This includes my politics. To say that Jesus is my Lord but attempt to withhold my political persuasions from Him is to steal that which is rightly His. I cannot keep what is no longer mine.[1] I must instead place all of me in His hands and allow Him to shape, reform, and refine me into His image. Challenging dinnertime conversations with Christian brothers and sisters, in which difficult topics are carefully thought through and explored, is a corporate way I can surrender my thinking to Him for refinement.

In the day of judgment, we will give an account for every word spoken.[2] This means, among many other things, that we will

---

[1] 1 Corinthians 6:19-20
[2] Matthew 12:36

give an account for our politics. We will give an account for what is spoken at our dinner tables. We will also give an account for how we chose to influence the course of history – whether we bravely spoke up and spoke out or shut down conversations in the name of 'peace.' If we withhold our politics from Him, we will have to explain why we allowed Jesus to transform *some* aspects of ourselves but refused Him access to others. There will be a reckoning with His eminent domain.

Such a Time as This

We live in a perilous moment. To shut down conversations and remain silent in the name of maintaining some temporary, artificial peace is to be apathetic to what is happening around us. Apathy is the opposite of Love. It has no place at the Christian table, especially not now.

Only years ago, I believed that the greatest threat to wisdom in the current age was the 'democratization of knowledge.'

What a nerdy phrase.

It means basically this: Anything we might wish to know is filtered and sorted in search engines and media platforms through the rule of popular opinion. Artificial intelligence fuels these engines. Information is displayed on our devices based on what AI has already determined *we* might like, sorted in priority based on what others have indicated that *they* like. Information is therefore made accessible to us not based on whether it is factually *true*, but whether it is *popular*. This is what some have called the 'democratization of knowledge.'

But now, technology is smarter than that. Rather than filtering information through popular opinion, it now filters it based exclusively on *our own* opinion. As if generating a reflection in our own narcissian pool, our personal search engines are now designed to produce search results that will reflect what each of us already believes to be true. The technology giants have lured us to worship the idol we love the most: our own ego. And in doing so, they have dulled our critical thinking skills and muddied any meaningful search for truth. Sadly, this is the means through which many of us currently consume content, form opinions, and perceive the world.

The downward spiral continues. There is an even *greater* threat to wisdom than the artificial intelligence that caters to our egos. Behind every major platform that the modern world uses to consume content, from social media to search engines to apps, is not only powerful, content-sorting AI but an even more powerful, content-filtering agenda that controls it. We are now living in an age of unprecedented global censorship, where anything published online or spoken in public forum is subject to immediate censorship by the media giants we foolishly rely on to post and consume content.

Actual wisdom and knowledge are now in grave danger. This elevates the importance of having local, personal political conversations.

The humble grassroots sharing of politics and news at the dinner table – perhaps one of the last domains of free thought – is mission-critical if we are to remain meaningfully aware, engaged, and influential in this chapter of history.

Taken together, engagement with politics at such a time as this is an essential Christian duty. Yes, it is *guaranteed* to make some dinners uncomfortable. For this reason, our conversations should be "*full of grace* and seasoned with salt."[1] But conversations absolutely *must* happen.

We could perhaps be a little more like my newly naturalized husband – willing to engage in taboo topics because he didn't think they were taboo at all. He simply believed it was important to know and to learn.

When the coffee turns cold and debate runs long, when current events take precedent over the dessert waiting in the fridge, when ideas are challenged and light bulbs come on,

---

[1] Colossians 4:6

Supper

when we realize the role we must play in the grand narrative of history, we are doing what great influencers like Jesus, our Founding Fathers, and countless others have done: discussing principles of polity.

As much as I don't like to admit it, my ever-curious, history-loving, taboo-immune husband is right.

"As many as I love, I rebuke and discipline. So be zealous and repent. Listen! I stand at the door and knock. If anyone hears my voice, and opens the door, I will come in to him and have dinner with him, and he with me."

Revelation 3:19-20 CSB

SUPPER

Dancing at the Dinner Table

I hear Your knock at the door and I know You've come,

not merely to greet me from the safe distance of the doorstep,

but to honor me

and risk Your reputation by coming inside

to dine at my table.

I open the door,

knowing full well that my house isn't fit to receive such a guest

but remembering that it was You who chose

to come and knock,

not me.

Kennedy

You could have dined on pristine mountaintops

or at the lavish tables of kings

but chose – for reasons Heaven holds – to come here

to dine with me instead.

Let's not waste a moment.

Come in and let's prepare this place.

I can't hide anything from You and my confessions loom long.

Dust is collecting on treasures You gave to me long ago

and chains are shackling promises You whispered once.

Idols sit high and polished on the mantle

and that pottery You shaped so lovingly for me

is shattered on the floor.

But You have come.

Open wide the windows

and let the fresh wind of Your Spirit blow freely through this place.

Supper

I know not where it comes from or where it is going,

but let it blow where it pleases here.

Turn the tables in your loving rage,

break the chains of shame

and destroy the shining idols – I never should have placed them there.

Restore the treasures You crafted

and the works of art You made.

Bring Your beauty back into this place.

Establish Your presence.

Let's not forsake a moment.

Come, let's sit together and eat.

Truly every good thing in this house came from You,

from the aromatics in the cupboard to the air in the room.

I have food

because You've provided it to me,

and now I get to share it back to You.

Kennedy

Such is your kindness,

that you ask nothing of me

other than what You Yourself have given.

And though it's all yours,

as I place dish after dish at our dinner table,

suddenly they are transformed by Your presence

into heavenly colors and flavors and smells.

I can almost taste the drink of Cana

as You transform water into wine in our cups.

So it is,

that all You've given me,

I set before You.

What I set before You,

You transform into something better

and set before me.

This is our dance at the table.

SUPPER

I continue to marvel.

What a miracle to have You here!

Your presence has power.

Every worry,

pain,

frustration,

hurt,

evil,

scheme

has faded into a forgotten and neglected silence.

Time has surrendered to irrelevance.

Here, at this table,

is just

You and me.

me and You.

Jesus, I've laid my best and my all before You.

Kennedy

The meal continues on,

and I search my house for more to serve.

Meanwhile,

You are going about Your own table-setting hospitality.

You are preparing a table before *me*

in the presence of my enemies,

ensuring my cup overflows,

ensuring I know that I am welcome.

So continues our dance at the dinner table.

Glory turns to glory,

glory surpasses glory.

We eat and we're satisfied.

I rest.

You smile.

I smile.

So goes our dance.

Supper

But none of this makes sense!

God who dwells in unapproachable light,

how could You fain to draw so near?

Why would you indulge to dance so far from heaven,

with one so small and far from You?

"Do not try to solve the mystery. Just stare at it."[1]

So I stare.

Marvel.

Wonder.

Embrace.

This is our dance

at the table.

---

[1] Francis Chan, *Letters to the Church* (Colorado Springs: David C. Cook, 2018).

For as heaven is higher than earth, so My ways are higher than your ways, and My thoughts than your thoughts.

Isaiah 55:9

Supper

Grief

Once I carried an unborn life whom no one knew. I named him *Isaiah*, not because I would have given him that name at his birth, but because it was the book I was reading at his death. Isaiah was knit, only partially, in his mother's womb and then, as if some work of art abandoned in the darkness of night, he was left unfinished.

My memories of him are soaked in tears and blood. Returning home from the hospital, I cradled his salvaged vestige of existence that had been wrapped tenderly by my husband in a small white cloth. A spiritual torment overtook the physical pain of miscarriage, born of a nauseating wave of guilt. I had delayed announcing him and we had only days before, on Christmas, revealed the big news to our daughters. Precious few had known he even existed. How could people possibly appreciate him now that he doesn't? I am his mother. How could I have let his existence go unknown until his existence was no more?

Losses should be grieved in community. Even the Holy Spirit, who grieves the supernatural losses evoked by our sinful ways, grieves in the precious company of Father and Son, in the community of the Trinity.[1] But what community can grieve an unborn, unknown child? I felt isolated and misunderstood, adrift in a sea of grief which I could not, or would not, let anyone else alleviate.

It was this existential struggle that was the unspoken backdrop of what happened next.

Solidarity

I do not know what went through his mind or why he made the offer. I do not know the hidden part of him that our miscarriage must have triggered. I do not even know how he knew to do what he did. But my uncle offered our little unformed baby to be buried on his land. And then, in an extravagant expression of solidarity, he offered to create a proper tombstone to memorialize him.

---

[1] Ephesians 4:30

Supper

My aunt and uncle live on a sprawling mountainside of untouched land that was acquired generations ago by our family. Far out of town, down an eroding gravel road, deep into the quiet of unvisited nature, there stands a cedar-planked house they call home. Not far away from the house, an unassuming footpath leads through trees, around a bend, and opens into a valley. The grass is green and grazed by cattle. A small pond sits still beneath the shade of an old, sturdy tree. This is the place he has chosen. A place of peace, reflection, and solitude.

A burial here would signal, to us and to the wider world, that he had existed.

Acceptance

The next morning, we were to lay our little one to rest in this valley of peace. Feeling helpless, out of sorts, and grasping for any ritual that might dignify and honor what was left of our son, I anointed him with frankincense and laid the tiny wrapping that held him carefully in a decorative box that would serve as his coffin. With my husband and our daughters, we drove under miserable gray skies through the winding country lanes and down the eroding gravel road. I met my uncle at the entrance of the discreet path that leads to the valley. He and my aunt had funeral flowers waiting for us.

He invited us to choose any place that suited us best. I chose a spot at the base of the time-beaten tree, with roots that must grow deep into the pond that sits beneath its branches.

"The man who trusts in the Lord, whose confidence indeed is the Lord, is blessed. He will be like a tree planted by water..."[1]

My husband began to dig. Prayers of hope and gratitude mixed with the burning salt of tears and the empty space of silence that hung over the valley. Moments later, as the last of the earth covered the trifling coffin, we stood in a circle, each helplessly confronting the unforgiving reality that we have no control over the things in life that permanently change us. Bitterness fought with peace for prominence in my spirit. My daughters were unsure of how to mourn or react to all of this; they tried to take their cues from me. My husband remained a pillar of strength, without which I would have crumbled and fallen apart.

FULFILLMENT

In the days that followed, my uncle would fulfill his promise to create a tombstone, on which he allowed me to choose the words. He is no mason and had no experience, but what he did have was heartfelt determination fueled by empathy. He

---

[1] Jeremiah 17:7-8

Supper

designed and built a frame and elicited the help of his son and friends to pour concrete, imprint lettering, and take the many other steps a tombstone requires. This was no simple task. It was a labor of love that took months to complete. All for a life he did not even know existed until it was gone.

I will never forget my uncle's kindness, which stands in contrast to the well-meaning consolation of so many other people. The world has a rather barren perspective on miscarriage that trivializes the pain of suffering mothers. People who turn to science and fate for sterile explanations on the matters of life give voice to feeble comments that are somehow expected to elicit comfort:

"This is just nature's way of correcting itself."

"These things just happen…"

"This is for the best."

But my uncle never offered sterile comfort. Instead, he instinctively did what Scripture compels us to do, which we often ignore or overlook, perhaps because we perceive it to be too simple and too difficult: *grieve with those who grieve.*[1]

In doing so, he shed healing light on my hidden, broken spirit. He then engaged the help of others to bring the tombstone to

---

[1] Romans 12:15

fruition, and in this he tenderly led a procession of community into my isolation. His actions said our child mattered. In defiance of the ways of the world, he affirmed the intrinsic value of a life unlived. And in dignifying my child, he dignified me.

Quite marvelously, he accomplished all of this without fully knowing the significance of what he was doing. This is a hallmark of a true disciple of Jesus, that their actions bring about supernatural healing and restoration without even realizing it.[1]

Mystery

Months later, he would be involved in an accident that would permanently damage his arm. As news of his uncertain fate and urgent race to the emergency room reached me in Florida, I found myself crying to the Lord for allowing the accident. I pleaded with Him, begged Him, stormed the throne room for a miracle.

You who knit him together in his mother's womb can knit him together again. Restore and reknit, remake the broken places. Bring about Your healing presence, Your mercy, Your grace. Repay the kindness he's shown.

---

[1] Matthew 25:31-46

Supper

After a very long, arduous, and pain-wracked journey which I could not possibly fathom, the Lord did answer our prayers. He provided healing and restored some functionality. But the arm that worked to create my unborn child's tombstone, the only evidence in the world that Isaiah ever existed, would not be the same in this life again.

I can't explain why my uncle's arm was mangled, or why my child was left unfinished. Perhaps these earthly losses are allowed so that our experience of heaven will be that much richer. No one will enjoy having two strong, healthy arms in heaven more than someone who knows what it's like to lose them on earth. And no parent will enjoy greeting their child in heaven as much as one who's buried him on earth.

Perhaps these pains were permitted as holy fires to refine us, burning away our pride, impatience, and illusions of control to deepen our mercy toward others and prepare us for the privileges and responsibilities of the world to come.

Perhaps, perhaps, perhaps. I could fill a book of *perhaps*, and even if they were all true, they could not exhaust the full reason and purpose behind it all. The wisdom of God holds mysteries that remain hidden and out of reach.[1]

---

[1] Isaiah 55:8-9

What I *do* know is enough for today. I do know that God is omniscient, omnipotent, and good. None of our tears or hardships, good deeds or mercies have escaped His watchful notice. He saw the redemptive power of my uncle's kindness to me. He heard the urgency in our emergency room prayers for him. He knows the intensity, the agony, the humanity of the various kinds of grief that we carry through life. And He promises to give ultimate purpose to all of it. He wastes none of our experience this side of heaven, all the while assuring us in divine whispers of mercy that 'this too shall pass.'

He does not give us complete answers for these deeper pains of life, but He does give us assurance:

"Tears may flow in the night, but joy comes in the morning."[1]

As Brother Lawrence memorably counsels us from four centuries past:

> *"Good when He gives, supremely good;*
> *Not less when He denies:*
> *Affliction, from His sovereign hand,*
> *Are blessings in disguise."*[2]

---

[1] Psalm 30:5 GNT
[2] Brother Lawrence, *The Practice of the Presence of God* (Peabody: Hendrickson Publishers, 2004).

SUPPER

"I am He,"
Jesus told her.

John 4:26

SUPPER

When Jesus Wasn't Hungry

The Gospel of John recounts a time when Jesus walked with His disciples from Judea to Galilee, inevitably passing through Samaria along the way. This northern journey would have taken several days, and Jesus arrived to a well in Samaria the way many travelers arrive to far-away places: tired and hungry.

Sending the disciples into town to buy food, Jesus sat by the well to rest. A woman fallen from social grace approached at noon, and He asked her for a drink of water.

Jesus, You broke through every social and political taboo when You held this outcasted, scandalized woman in Your gaze and asked her for help. What I love the most is that You genuinely needed her for that drink. You, the image of the

Invisible God, the Ancient of Days, the Bread of Life chose to humble Yourself to be in legitimate need of a woman who knew herself only as a disgrace.

This woman was going to the well alone in the heat of the day because she had sinned and chosen a path that was not God's. The community of women who would have been her water-fetching companions in the cool of the morning offered no neighborly company in the wake of her scandals.

It's radical to consider that the only reason she encountered Jesus that day, whom she wasn't even looking for, was because she had rejected God's ways for her life, was rejected by the community as a result, and had to go to the well alone. Her promiscuity, rebellion, and subsequent alienation paved her road. God went out of His way to find her there, ask for a drink of water, and reveal Himself to her.

Jesus, to this fallen woman who was lost to the ways of the world, You chose to reveal Your radical theology of missions, in which the giver is so humbled that he first needs the receiver, and the receiver is so dignified that she can first help the giver.

To her who was rejected by both the religious elite and her own people, You chose to reveal the true nature of worship. You care nothing for religious rituals or earned righteousness, but call us in Spirit and Truth to "the most selfless emotion of which our nature is capable."[1]

To this woman who knew only cheapened intimacy, You chose to reveal Yourself for the first time in the Gospel narratives as the great I AM. You looked past all that might separate her from You, and shared with her real intimacy by telling her Your true nature. You chose to be known intimately by someone who could little know herself.

To this woman You were vulnerable and risked that she would reject You.

The woman wasn't quick to embrace Jesus. She argued with Him, challenged His claims, and guarded herself.

Father Ephrem the Syrian, a fourth century theologian insightfully charted their discourse:

"At the beginning of the conversation, Jesus did not make Himself known to her, but first she caught sight of a thirsty man, then a Jew, then a Rabbi, afterwards a prophet, last of all the Messiah. She tried to get the better of the thirsty man, she showed dislike of the Jew, she heckled the Rabbi, she was swept off her feet by the prophet, and she adored the Christ."

---

[1] William Temple, Archbishop of Canterbury

The woman's response to her encounter with Jesus was to return to her town and evangelize the very people who had outcasted her. They listened. Scripture recounts that "they made their way toward Him" because of her.[1]

Jesus, You profoundly dignified her and then empowered her as the first female evangelist.

In a bold defiance of convention, Jesus ultimately used the sin-stained, broken path of this woman to reach not only her, but her neighbors too.

As a divine iconoclast, He shattered the way this woman thought about the nature of God and her role in His plan. Her shameful story became the sacred space in which her neighbors might draw close to Jesus.

It is outrageous to consider that You would allow sin to play a role in Your ultimate mission. You never condoned sinfulness and held that this woman's lifestyle was wrong. But Your mercy is so deep, Your power so great, Your victory over sin so complete that You can and will use what she's done wrong - what we've done wrong – to reach us.

"As in Paradise, God walks the Scriptures in search of man."[2]

---

[1] John 4:30
[2] Bishop Ambrose of Milan

Supper

You walked the desert to far-away places in search of her and those You'd reach through her; You walk the desert to far-away places in search of us and those You'll reach through us.

"There are a million ways to shatter the image of God, and only one way to restore it."[1]

Jesus.

The way. The truth. The life.

Giver of scandalous grace.

The "Great Iconoclast" who shatters all that's false and goes to great lengths to restore all that's true.[2]

And then, at long last, the disciples returned from the town bearing food. But Jesus, satisfied as He was that He'd found the one He'd searched for in the desert, wasn't hungry anymore.[3]

---

[1] Rosaria Butterfield, *The Secret Thoughts of an Unlikely Convert: An English Professor's Journey Into Christian Faith* (Pittsburgh: Crown & Covenant Publications, 2014).
[2] C.S. Lewis, *A Grief Observed* (London: Faber and Faber Limited, 1963).
[3] John 4:1-34

He unleashes His winds, and the waters flow.

Psalm 147:18

SUPPER

The Truth About Christians

A terrible rumor can circulate in places where Christianity has enjoyed a generation or two of widespread favor. It's whispered into the breeze of small towns, broadcast on the silver screens of big theatres, planted in the backyards of fenced homes, and surreptitiously entertained in the space between Sundays. The rumor lingers despite what the elders might think or what the Bible might say. It tempts, and taunts, and tries to draw the wandering heart away. It takes root easily in the minds of those who were born into Christian homes, growing in the imagination like an invasive weed to obscure the Gospel's beauty. It's a rumor I've known among my own kin and in my own mind.

It starts out simple, something a child might say because he doesn't want to get dressed up and go to church:

This is boring.

But then the rumor grows.

A 'yes' to Jesus is an automatic 'no' to everything enjoyable. Christians have the funereal life sentence of piety, forgoing the 'good life' in which everyone else seems to indulge, forced to watch all the action from the sidelines and never knowing what the exhilaration of real living feels like. To be a Christian is to be buttoned up, grayed, settled and safe. To gain Christ is to miss out on everything but hymnals and potlucks.

So very, very boring.

Surely there is more to the world out there! Many a "Christian kid" has left stale wooden pews to find it.

THOU SHALT NOT

This rumor about the dull, 'less than' life that is the dismal fate of Christians has spread too easily in Bible-belt communities, in part because the core of Jesus' message is often shrouded in an overbearing list of 'thou shalt not's.' In the legalistic spirit of the Pharisees from whom Jesus relentlessly distanced Himself, Christianity has become known more for what we shouldn't do than for what we should.

Religion is good at corroding the luster of life with lists of rules. But Jesus taught that we should live life in all its fullness. Rather than retreat behind the walls of overbearing rules, He taught that the way to worship God was by going out and *truly living*.

"Love the Lord your God with all your heart and with all your soul and with all your strength and with all your mind; and Love your neighbor as yourself... Do this and you will live." [1]

Instead of summarizing the Law with a list of things we *shouldn't do*, Jesus spoke in terms of what we *should do*. He said the key to life eternal is to love God and love your neighbor as yourself.[2] This brilliant distillation of the ancient Law establishes the order and richness of the full-color life that Jesus invites us into, and it does so in positive terms.

THOU *SHALL*

First, we are to love God.

He commands us to love Him with our heart. This is an invitation to make God the redeeming center of our desires, dreams, relationships, works of art, expressions of love.

---
[1] Luke 10:27-28
[2] Luke 10:25-37

He commands us to love Him with our soul. This is a visceral appeal to engage in the transcendent: worship, mindfulness, delight, faith, hope, and prayer.

He commands us to love Him with our mind. This is a call to creatively ground our studies, business, reasoning, discoveries, and struggles in the singular pursuit of God's glory.

He commands us to love Him with our strength. This is a challenge to steward our bodies, health, abilities, and age-earned wisdom with an aim to manifest His Kingdom on earth, as it is in Heaven.

In this commandment, He invites us to worship God in every moment of every day, to be consumed by His glory as evidenced in every aspect of our life and creation, to recognize that worship is a way of life that cannot fit into a timeslot on Sunday but that permeates all our existence.

Then, we are told to love ourselves so that we'll be able to love our neighbors.

We are often broken in two ways as we relate to one another: we selfishly pursue our own interests while ignoring others, making idols of ourselves; or we fix our attention so much on others that we neglect and even demean ourselves with an ill-informed understanding of humility. In a single command,

Jesus brilliantly addresses both sins by inviting us to love each of His image-bearers with equal passion: ourselves and our neighbors. He invites us to recognize our God-given dignity, to invest the time to love and care for ourselves, and then commands us to pour that same love into the lives of others.

Run Wild

The Christian life is saying yes to life-giving things and no to life-stealing things. It is far greater than a list of things we shalt not do. It is not stoic or gray. It lacks no good thing. The Greatest Commandment on which the entire Christian life rests – to love God and love neighbor as self – offers exponential opportunities for adventure.

As a kid, I entertained the lie that living for Jesus is boring and restrictive. I felt that rumor grow to choke out my enthusiasm for a life of holiness, turning my gaze to the tempting exploits and carnivalesque diversions of the outside world. I bought into the lie that I was missing out.

By grace, it was indulgence in the cheap, imposter thrills of the wider world that helped me realize I was wrong. The enemy can offer what glitters, but he cannot offer what's gold.

As an adult, I have determined to put my faith into action and live the adventure Christ offers to His followers. I once helped sneak a hundred wedding gowns into Cuba. I led my kids through a riotous Paraguayan prison. I worshiped with the church on five continents. I studied amid the storied spires of Oxford. I walked a pilgrimage with friends across the Spanish countryside. I toasted smores with students on a Guatemalan volcano. I prayed with a woman in the ice cream aisle until the manager interrupted us because the supermarket was closing. I warred in spiritual places and felt the darkness give way to unrelenting Light. All this was born of a life truly lived.

The rumor about Christianity being a life of missing out, sadly believed by so many of us, cannot bear the weight of lived experience. If my life is one small example, it is evidence that Christianity is anything but boring. It is rich, colorful, risky, and surprising. It is purposeful. Every adventure that decorates my existence has been orchestrated *by* Jesus, *with* Jesus, and *for* Jesus. He writes the best stories, and I wouldn't trade Him for anything.

As for the things we Christians *shalt not do*, I confess that they are many, and that I've grown to find this good. The boundaries God has placed around the Christian life are not designed to restrict us or withhold anything good from us, but "to give room for good things to run wild."[1] The boundaries are in place to protect our freedoms, so that we'll be able to

---

[1] G.K. Chesterton, *Orthodoxy* (Peabody: Hendrickson Publishers Marketing, LLC, 2006).

embark – unhindered and unafraid – on the next adventure Jesus has planned.

We are told not to worship any other gods. This is (in part) because any false god will leave us frustrated and unfulfilled at best, and enslaved at worst. We are told not to lie. This is because those who lie become slaves to those lies, and Jesus wants us to be free. We are told not to covet. Jealousy keeps us from being able to fully enjoy what God has given specially to us. We are told not to boast. Bragging sets us up to fall into humiliation when our vulnerabilities get the best of us.

I'm grateful for the things God tells me not to do. When I cross the threshold into temptation, they never deliver the pleasure the devil promises but always ensnare me and weigh me down. They hold me back. To sin is to lose my freedom, dull my senses, enslave my spirit.

Jesus wants me to be free, and He wants me to be full. He once described the Kingdom of Heaven as a King throwing a great Wedding Feast,[1] inviting all who would come to enjoy the richest meats and finest wines.[2] He invites us, in His Greatest Commandment, to come to that Feast, to taste and see that He

---

[1] Matthew 22:2
[2] Isaiah 25:6

is good,[1] to live according to His order, and to discover what it means to truly live.

---

[1] Psalm 34:8

SUPPER

Jesus shouted, "Lazarus, come out!" the dead man came out... "Loose him & let him go."

John 11:43-44

SUPPER

Through Sugarcane and Tobacco

"Jesus wept."[1]

He stood at His friend's grave, surrounded by mourners who accused Him of arriving too late. Jesus, the Author of life, found Himself in a world plagued by of death.

In His humanness, He stared into the face of death and wept.

He was very far from Home.

Growing up, the island nation of Cuba was an anomaly out of reach, exotic and unknowable beyond the stories of revolution captured in black and white photos in my textbooks. I never

---

[1] John 11:35

dreamed of traveling there, but the Lord's dreams are always bigger than mine. He has granted us not only multiple passages into Cuba, but endearing family who faithfully wait in the sun while we suffer the racketeering of Cuban customs, always rejoicing to greet us when we make it to the open air and peculiar world of Cuba on the other side.

My husband and I recently took a weekend trip to Havana to visit our two dearest local friends. The time was intended to be refreshing and refueling for all four of us. This meant we would have to surrender our respective cultural burdens to the Lord: we would let go of the American preoccupation with time and they would let go of the Cuban preoccupation with money. We would bridge two foreign worlds. The idea was to weekend together unrushed (on Latin time), and unconcerned with finances (on American money). In a rare opportunity for strategic cultural exchange, we would each enjoy the best of how the other lived.

On the Sunday of our special weekend, we ventured to Pinar del Rio, where our friend's mother lives. Entering her house was a surreal moment. As if stepping through some vortex, I suddenly felt like I was no longer in the very different world of Cuba, but sitting in the very familiar world of Arkansas.

Supper

Her simple house was appointed with minimal country-style furnishings. An oval dining table sat just off her small kitchen. Art that her son had painted hung on the walls. We gathered around her dining table to look at family photos and share stories while our friend helped his beloved mamá cook lunch.

Flipping through old albums while straining to translate the anecdotes that rolled off native tongues, I stopped when I came to a faded photo of an old man dressed in overalls, sitting in a simple chair outside a small wooden house. He wore a farmer's hat. He was bent over a Bible that lay open in his lap, reading under the shade of a tree in the middle of the day.

Wait. I know this man. I know this picture. I've seen it somewhere before.

But where?

Back home.

I saw in this photo those relatives whom I know and also never met; whose pictures are piled into an old trunk in my grandmother's bedroom. I held the photo of the humble farmer reading his Bible in the shade and thought how it belonged in that trunk. This was a photo of my great uncle, my great grandfather, my rural relatives of ages past. How could it be here in Cuba? How could I recognize my kin in a world so very far away?

The foreignness of Cuba dissipated in the face of the familiar. We are more alike than we are different.

Our humble host laid out a princely feast by Cuban standards: creole chicken, congee, fried yucca, fried plantains, fresh sliced tomatoes, sweetened Cuban coffee, and Raidel's childhood favorite, dulce de papaya. The local produce may have been different from the squash and okra back home, but they were fried in a grandmother's kitchen all the same. The dessert may have been more tropical than the banana pudding back home, but it was handmade by a mother wanting to please her son all the same. The stories we told at the table may have been tinged with the hardships of communism, but they were filled with laughter and reminiscence all the same. Somehow, someway, everything in this experience felt cozy and familiar. It all felt mysteriously the same as what I've always known.

Even our friend's mother, who so graciously prepared our meal, resonated such a familiar and homey presence. She was a daughter, a mother, a grandmother. She carried scars and shame, stories and sacrifices. She sang similar songs, proclaimed the same savior. She was sweet and generous, reserved and discreet. She harbored painful secrets from her past. Her eyes hid her suffering. She cooked the foods her children loved and waited patiently for them to pay her visits.

Supper

She appeared to be a fine Southern woman if I ever met one. But she is not Southern at all. She is Cuban.

As we drove back to Havana with hearts and stomachs full, I stared out the window into the black, star-studded sky, still musing over the way her house felt like home and the transient nature of our perceived cultural differences. We drove through vast stretches of tobacco and sugarcane fields not unlike the soybean and rice fields that sprawl across the Arkansas landscape outside my grandmother's home. We whizzed past farm after farm, and our friend filled in the gaps of our understanding, recounting the story of his mother's hard life.

Her history shined a spotlight on something she had said earlier in the day. Small and frail, now reaching into her eighties and unable to work, I had asked her how she spends her time. She responded simply, "Very well."

This is a profound reply from a woman whose story I now learned was plagued with abandonment from childhood, paternal and spousal abuse, and a depth of despair so hopeless that her own relatives had encouraged her to commit suicide. They had looked down upon her hopeless existence, saw only shards of a broken life, and found no reason she should keep living.

On the day she had planned to kill herself, her small children miraculously came down with a fever. They needed her to nurse them back to health. Already fatherless and despised by relatives, she knew that if she did not care for them, no one would. She put her suicide plans aside and took up her duties as a mother. Their sickness saved her life.

As the days passed, her depression subsided enough to make life seem livable again. Her obligations to her offspring pulled her forward, sunrise to sunrise, sunset to sunset. She did not thrive, but she existed. She endured.

Time passed in the eternal summer of Cuba. From scandal she birthed her youngest son. He grew up hungry, sheltered by a small shack and his mother's love. Life was hard.

This was the long-past suffering her eyes had hidden as we dined at her table that afternoon.

Eventually the endless tobacco and sugarcane ended, giving way to plantain fields. Riding through vast stretches of farmland in unobstructed night has a special way of creating space for the mind to think. And think I did: *Where was Jesus in this horrible story?*

Supper

"Jesus wept."

He stood at His friend's grave, surrounded by mourners who didn't, who wouldn't, who couldn't possibly understand. He was not weeping because His friend had temporarily passed into death – He knew the miracle of life that He was about to bring about for Lazarus. Rather, He saw beyond the tomb and stared into the spiritual abyss of death, destruction, darkness, and despair that the enemy had heaped onto the world He'd created and it made Him angry. He contorted His face for the grimacing pain that burned in His heart and He wept, with passion and fury, at what the devil had done, at what humanity helped the devil do, at the ways we have separated ourselves from Him.

In His divinity, He stared into the face of death and wept.

And then He rose to create beauty from the ashes of the enemy's fires. He redeemed the path of Lazarus. He spoke Life where there was once Death.

That youngest son she had birthed and toiled to raise eventually grew up. He took an unlikely path for a child born in an atheist state: he became a preacher.

In the first sermon he ever preached, his mother was there to show her support. Indigenous witchcraft mixed with remnants of imported Catholicism had shaped her religious practice up to that day. To her son's surprise and eternal delight, she raised her hand at the invitation to receive Jesus as her savior. Her hand would be the first he ever saw raise in his evangelism ministry.

He would go on to preach hundreds of sermons across the island. He would preach to thousands on American soil and hundreds in a Paraguayan prison. He would traverse every possible road in the oppressed nation of Cuba, bringing the Good News of Jesus Christ. His prayers would give way to miracles and his preaching would give way to revivals as the Holy Spirit moved through his obedience. He would become a bold leader in the Church that the Communists were known to fear. He would become a faithful brother and confidant, a pastor in troubled times and a fire to wake the sleeping. He would concern himself with following Jesus and leading his family. And he would vow to take care of his mother.

This life, so full of influence and blessing, would not have existed except for the sin-stained, death-riddled path his mother endured that led to his birth.

Supper

Her suffering (and quite scandalously, even her sin) was not in vain, because Jesus redeemed it all in her story, in the life of her son, in the lives of everyone Christ reaches through her story and his ministry, and in countless other ways not known to us this side of heaven. He used it *all* for her good, for our good, and for His glory.[1]

As with Lazarus, so with our friend's mother. As with her, so with us.

Nearing Havana in the deep of the night, that youngest son of hers continued driving us faithfully toward our lodging. I stared up at the glistening expanse of cosmos hanging out of reach, marveling at the grace and blessings Jesus had and would continue to pour forth from this woman's broken life.

I counted myself among those who have been blessed, and I rejoiced in the homey familiarity of the story we'd heard. This same Jesus who gave redemptive purpose to her sin and suffering has done and will do the same for mine. *There is hope.*

Fatigued from the day's adventures and night's reflections, I lifted a prayer of thanksgiving for our Cuban friends – our family – and smiled at the satisfaction of this mission

---

[1] **Romans 8:28**

accomplished. Together, we had experienced what we set out to do that weekend: live the best of both our worlds. But we were wrong to think this had something to do with time or money. The true *best* of both our worlds, the bridge that brought us together, is the one God we worship, the Jesus who wept.

Supper

Jesus Himself came near and began to walk along with them.

Luke 24:15

SUPPER

An Afternoon Walk

A long way from home there is a sacred space called Monserrate that sits 10,431 feet above sea level. From here, one observes the pristine beauty of the Andes Mountains on one side and the thief-riddled metropolis of Bogotá on the other, with a white church devoted to *el Señor Caído* bridging between them. The entire mission of Christ seems to express itself here, where the creation of God meets the creation of man in the person of Jesus.

I love this place, and I pilgrimage here at every opportunity God provides. It is a place to meander high above the city noise and indulge in quintessential Colombian comfort. Nearing the top, one can smell giant ears of corn sizzling over open fires, hand-stuffed tamales and cheesy-sweet arepas waiting to be tasted. Artisans serve up hot chocolate with wedges of fresh cheese and family recipes of herbal teas infused with coca leaves for altitude sickness. It is a feast for the soul and the senses.

At the top of Monserrate is the *Viacrucis*, the Way of the Cross. I have walked this particular *Viacrucis* many times but have never entered into it. Its significance was lost on me until now. This time I walked with fresh scars from a war I cannot see. In this vulnerable state, my clichéd worship of Christ for His Passion, which has characterized my mindset for every prior *Viacrucis,* was halted by my shock in what I saw in the shadow of each station: myself.

The truth became suddenly and disturbingly clear, that my personal experience of sin and death – the *human experience* – is a mere shadow of the hard-stone ultimate reality of Jesus' experience at Calvary. All I have known of life, I have lived only in part. Jesus lived it in full.

Pilate Condemns Jesus to Die

Jesus is accused, judged, mocked, abused, rejected and hurt by both believers and nonbelievers, by people who knew Him and people who didn't. He endures the full concatenation of events that can possibly follow sin. And then He is stripped naked. He knows the shame of nakedness that occurs when our sins are laid bare before the delight and mockery of others.

His complete suffering of the consequences of sin and death gives way to an intimacy between us that only shared experience can establish. He understands my suffering more than I do because He bore the full weight of it, and the *Viacrucis* challenges me to see Him living my full suffering.

It feels sacrilegious to suggest I have a shared experience of suffering with God Himself, and yet, this scandal of the Gospel persists. I really am there, at each station in the *Viacrucis*, living a mere shadow of Jesus' ultimate reality.

There is much to be discovered in that lot of life we share with God.

JESUS ACCEPTS HIS CROSS

He remains calm in the crucible of sin. He offers no excuses to defend Himself, even though an army of angels could have rightfully come to His defense.[1] My heart is silent as I suddenly recall the instructions He made clear to me months ago, in my own crucible, not to defend or excuse myself, but rather to trust in the Holy Spirit as my sole defense.[2] I realize now that His instructions to me were birthed at Calvary. My

---

[1] Matthew 26:53
[2] John 16:7

personal affliction is in His shadow; it is suddenly light and temporary.[1]

Jesus Falls for the First Time

He falls down while carrying the cross. The Viacrucis depicts Jesus falling three times. Each time He falls I recall the ancient Scripture teaching that the righteous will fall seven times and rise again.[2] Jesus is truly righteous, and He falls carrying the weight of sin. He knows the pain of falling down, the humiliation of others seeing Him fall, and the need for the Father's strength to lift Him up again.

Simon Helps Carry the Cross

He is also helped along the way. No one understands completely what He alone endures, but in the Father's mercy, some are there to tend to Him. Jesus experiences community even in the loneliness of His ultimate work, and in doing so He corroborates the high value I have instinctively placed on the saints God has called to surround me in my suffering. He knows when a friend is worth more than life.[3]

Veronica Wipes the Face of Jesus

---

[1] 2 Corinthians 4:17
[2] Proverbs 24:16
[3] John 15:13

Veronica is nowhere recorded in the Scriptures and yet her role in the story has been etched in literal stone and propagated the world over since medieval times. This embellishment of Jesus' story exists because the Catholic Church, by its own admission, sought to explain a relic with the markings of the purported face of Christ. Even at this historically objectionable station, I see myself in its shadow. Jesus knows what it is for His experience of suffering to be distorted by alternate agendas, gossip, blind eyes, and deaf ears. Jesus knows intimately the pain that sears us when our deepest suffering is caricatured or twisted to fit someone else's *a priori* assumptions. Jesus was the embodiment of Truth itself, and yet the truth about Him is rarely told. He endures.

JESUS DIES ON THE CROSS

My mind is flooded with the extraordinary life of the historical Jesus as I stare at Him dead.

This is the Jesus who laughed with His friends, who turned water into wine at a wedding[1] and who empowered underdogs.[2] This is the Jesus who was accused of eating too much and feasting with sinners.[3] The Jesus who was bold,

---

[1] John 2:1-11
[2] Mark 1:40-45
[3] Matthew 11:19

confronting power dynamics and corruption among political leaders.[1] This is the Jesus who healed the sick[2] and brought the dead back to life,[3] who was once so delighted to minister to a woman at the well that He forgot He was hungry.[4] He did so much good that the world cannot contain enough books to record it all.[5] This is the Jesus who knew the richness and goodness of truly living and being fully alive, who was anointed with the oil of Joy because He loved righteousness and hated evil.[6] This is the Jesus I am waiting to drink wine with some day.[7] But He now lays lifeless.

To my horror, I see in the deceased Christ what I was blind to until experiencing some shadow of it myself: His joy is gone.

Jesus knows what it is for a full-color life to be robbed of joy and turn gray and lifeless. He knows what it is for the enemy to steal, kill and destroy a person's strength and livelihood.

And He knows the casualty of the enemy's battles. That little life caught in the crossfire of my unseen war, which could not

---

[1] Luke 13:6-9
[2] Matthew 17:14-18
[3] John 11:38-44
[4] John 4:31-34
[5] John 21:25
[6] Hebrews 1:9
[7] Isaiah 25:6

survive within me, is a shadow of the Larger-Than-Life within Him that did not survive the war either.

I cannot take my eyes off this carnage of a life lost; realizing He, too, has lived my nightmare, that in reality He knows my grief more than I do.

"Surely I am with you always, Kara."[1]

He Himself comes, takes me by the hand, and does what I cannot do myself: moves me past this death, and to the next station.

JESUS IS RESURRECTED

I have come to the victorious image of the resurrected Christ, whose joy is now free and impermeable, epitomizing hope for the broken saints of every generation.

Having fully experienced my sin and death, He does the unthinkable, inviting me to fully experience His Shalom wholeness and life.[2]

The *Viacrucis* is a path. It is a walk through the valley of the shadow of my own death. It is a testament to the reality that

---

[1] Matthew 28:20
[2] Psalm 103:3-5

death is the only way to resurrection. And a reminder to us all that the fuller the death, the greater the resurrection life.

I don't want to leave this mountain top. But the *Viacrucis* is a path that continues, and so must I. Jesus reminds me, as my friends come back into focus and the clock resumes its march against the agenda of the day, that He too knows what it is to leave the safety of the mountaintop, to walk into the filth and the danger of the city below.

I take one last look at this fifteenth station, the Resurrected Christ standing in strength and power. He invites me to see myself there, too, living in the shadow of Himself, the Overcomer.[1]

---

[1] John 16:33

SUPPER

So go into the highways & byways, & invite everyone you find to the wedding feast.

Matthew 22:9 TLV

Supper

Wedding Invitations

A memoir from a day on mission in Paraguay.

Yesterday a young man was murdered upon arrival at Tacumbú prison. But the sun rises on a new day as if he never lived. Human filth and excrement weigh the air like a tangible stronghold, fueling the invisible tyrant of hopelessness that reigns and roams here. A military tank guards the entrance while a screaming woman outside is outraged to be denied visitation. But hungry prostitutes are welcomed to peddle their wares - fake breasts and men's beards on tired bodies masked with smiles. Nothing makes sense here.

Into this swirling orgy of darkness, thirteen newly baptized brides scorn the shame and boldly enter. Today is their wedding day. Inside, thirteen redeemed men, whose crimes span marijuana to murder and whom Jesus proudly calls His own, are waiting. They've done their best to wash away evidence of prison as they don borrowed suits and new ties, a wedding gift donated by saints a world away who will never know them this side of Heaven.

Mockery from intoxicated criminals is drowned out by the sophisticated beauty of our friend Javier's sax. The ambiance of the prison is transformed – if only for a moment – by the audacious intentionality of a group of saints who are hell-bent on ushering light into dark places.

Heaven leans in to witness this far-fetched celebration of two becoming one. Husbands receive their brides in these humblest of circumstances, and those who know Jesus pause to consider that this wedding is a shadow of the Great Wedding to come. That God would scandalize Himself by using this unlikely occasion to tell His own story, and point us toward His wedding in Heaven, is an impossible idea to all except those who know that God glories to do impossible things.

Supper

He does not seem to mind His wedding invitations being given out freely in Tacumbú. He glories in it.

And having reveled in bringing hope into the poverty of prison, He does not forget the opposite echelon of Paraguayan society, those plagued by poverty of spirit.

As the sun sets on this very same day, doctors and lawyers, culture-shapers and influencers draped in dazzling floor-length gowns and black suits, hiding behind the protective facade of high fashion and diamonds, make their entrance at the World Trade Center.

Mingling in their midst - and unbeknownst to them - is a Tacumbú prisoner who was granted a weekend of freedom by the order of a well-meaning judge and the decree of a sovereign God. For the first time ever he is taking his wife, whom he met and married in prison, on a romantic date.

Fresh flowers and meticulously arranged charcuterie on heirloom wood displays blend with candlelight, champagne flutes and Bossa Nova sounds to signal to all that a special evening is upon us. Paraguay's most notable chef hones his art in four inspired courses while a group of traveling saints share their battle-won wisdom about marriage in four inspired talks.

All buffers are stripped away as couples look to one another in the intimacy of their private tables. The atmosphere is set.

Food for the body and food for the heart are served. In this carefully crafted sacred space, they hold a mirror to their marriage, their lives, their hearts. They are challenged to empty their past and present hurts before a timeless and merciful God, to examine their order of priorities against the order set by heaven, to build their home on the Rock that promises to both shape and secure them, and to risk their finest treasures to invest in a marriage that flourishes under the blessings of God. While sitting comfortably amidst the trivial treasures of this world, they are offered a glimpse of the Divine Treasures of Heaven, whose shine no measure of life's storms can dull.

Here, too, God scandalizes Himself to tell His story and point us toward His wedding in Heaven. He does not seem to mind His wedding invitations being given out freely among the spiritually poor at the gala in the World Trade Center. He glories in it.

As the clock strikes midnight, the missionaries pause, feet aching from the day's journey traversing Paraguayan society for Jesus. They laugh together and delight to recall the fingerprints of God over every detail of the day, eagerly recollecting the moments of Holy Spirit-fueled transformation they witnessed in hearts and minds.

Supper

Behind the excited chatter of joy rendered by a mission accomplished, there is a silent, sacred space in each of their hearts that *remembers:* God scandalized Himself by using their worst moments and their battle scars to tell His own story and point us toward His wedding in heaven.

God does not seem to mind His wedding invitation being given out freely among this group of poor dreamers who call themselves the *Global Marriage Mission*. He glories in it.

But we are citizens of Heaven, where the Lord Jesus Christ lives.

Philippians 3:20 NLT

Supper

Happy Hunting Grounds

"Well when I kick the bucket…"

I can't count how many sentences start off like this. As a kid, Granny used to disturb my naïve understanding of life with her casual anticipation of death. For as long as I can remember, she has been looking forward to her "happy hunting grounds" with a determination that makes the rest of us, whose faith in the eternal promises of God pales in comparison to her own, unsure and disconcerted.

Granny understands a truth that many of us do not want to face: she doesn't belong here. She was created for a place that was created just for her, and the present earth is not it. She is a citizen of heaven.

This understanding gives her a quiet and deeply rooted strength. Beneath her meek veneer one finds a steady power, the ability to withstands storms with the inner wisdom that renders the worst of life's torments futile and temporary.

She can enjoy, but is largely detached from, the niceties and "little purties" of life, knowing that even the greatest of earthly luxuries will appear rusted and moth-eaten compared to the eternal beauties that adorn the place that Jesus has prepared for her.[1]

Determined to leave no ties to this fading-away place, she has already written off much of what she owns. Behind decorative plates and picture frames, inside books and on the tags of pillows, scattered all throughout her home one can find the carefully written cursive name of the person who will own that item after her, usually the person who originally gave it to her. In this way, she is already returning to this life all that belongs to it, knowing that she will soon have no use for them.

Oh, how I used to resent her faith in heaven. I rejected it because I could never understand it. She longs for "happy hunting grounds." What's so *happy* about *hunting* anyway?

---

[1] John 14:3

Supper

Like the rest of my extended and close-knit family, I wanted to keep her here with us as long as possible. I would struggle to see the names written on the back of everything. I didn't care whose name was written (bickering over inheritance isn't my thing). I didn't like seeing the names because they were each poignant reminders of the unwelcome reality of her impending death, about which she is the only one who could possibly be happy.

One day, when Granny's zeal for her "happy hunting grounds" was very far from my mind and I was least expecting to change my perspective on anything, God made His move. I was perusing the shelves of a bookstore when a stranger interrupted my quiet entertainment and encouraged me to read the *Chronicles of Narnia*. The complete set was on sale for $1.99. *Where did this guy come from, and why is he giving me book tips?* I took stock of his determination, went blank trying to think of a polite refusal, and judged I would look cheap for turning down such an obvious bargain on a literary classic, so I relented. I threw *The Chronicles of Narnia* in my basket, to appease the stranger and return to my peaceful perusing, if for nothing else.

Many months passed.

Eventually, that book made it to the top of my leaning tower of books waiting to be read. I was still questioning my decision to purchase a children's story under a stranger's pressure when I read the opening lines.

"This is a story about something that happened long ago..."

In only a few pages, the world of Narnia came alive. This timeless work, penned by atheist-turned-Christian C.S. Lewis, was an unexpected coup. God stole into my reason by way of my imagination.

What surprised me the most was the impact that the last chapter of the last book, aptly titled *The Last Battle,* had on my worldview. The epic saga culminates in death being swallowed up in life. I remember wishing the 767-page story was a hundred pages longer as I neared the end. In a rapture of the imagination, I was caught up in every word that formed the characters' magnificent journey deeper into heaven, and suddenly realized that I longed to join them.

> *"... the things that began to happen after that were so great and beautiful that I cannot write them. And for us this is the end of all the stories, and we can most truly say that they all lived happily ever after. But for them it was only the beginning of the real story. All*

> *their life in this world and all their adventures in Narnia had only been the cover and the title page: now at last they were beginning Chapter One of the Great Story which no one on earth has read: which goes on for ever: in which every chapter is better than the one before."*

I closed the book in stunned silence. God, through the creative genius of Lewis, had accomplished an impossible feat: in a most curious and unusual turn of events, He had made me look forward to my own death.

Lewis' story-telling "baptized my imagination," to borrow a phrase from his own Christian journey.[1]

This is when I finally understood Granny's determination for the grave. When the Lord calls her Home, our shared faith will become her personal reality. She will at last begin "Chapter One of the Great Story." She will not teary to look back on the broken world or the trivial things she has left behind. She will behold the Author of her faith,[2] praise Him for leading her from death into resurrection life,[3] and rest in the warmth and

---

[1] C.S. Lewis, *Surprised by Joy* (New York: Inspirational Press, 1986).
[2] Hebrews 12:2
[3] John 5:24

solace of being Home.[1] She will take up the adventures He's set before her, taste the wine she's never known before,[2] enjoy unspeakable beauties and full-color life.[3] She will be caught up in the joys of ruling and reigning with the King.[4] She will be in the place for which she was made.

She will have finally arrived to her "happy hunting grounds"... though precisely what it is she will be *hunting* in *heaven* is anyone's guess.

---

[1] Hebrews 13:14
[2] Matthew 26:29
[3] 1 Corinthians 2:9
[4] 2 Timothy 2:12

Supper

These are a shadow of the things that were to come; the reality, however, is found in Christ.

Colossians 2:17 NIV

SUPPER

Signposts

Laughter and indulgence epitomize our family gatherings. Stories of bygone days conspire with the aroma of homecooked meals to lure us to the table and keep us there for hours, always eager to hear just one more tale and regretful when the hour of farewell imposes itself upon our fun.

My favorites have always been my dad's, whose effortless spinning of tales is an endearing convocation of humorous impersonations, building anticipation, and purposeful pause that holds any audience captive. His artful storytelling awakens the oral traditions of old, harkening back to ancient times of ceremony and bonfires and starlight. In my eyes, he is the keeper of our rich heritage of memories and guardian of the joy that holds our family roots together.

As kids we would often ask him to retell his stories that we had canonized as classics: adventures in the wooded horizon of Little Rock in the days before they built the bridge over the Arkansas River; legendary mishaps as a summer camp counselor with unruly children; triumphs as a black belt, lone pole vaulter, and #23 footballer; and practical jokes at the unwitting expense of his brothers and childhood friends. The stories are vintage but they never age, and I never tire of hearing them.

And then there are the equally relished stories of our humble, home-grown heroes to whose greatness we could only hope to aspire: our grandfather the self-taught architect living the American dream with his sweetheart, our great uncle choosing a lifetime of singleness over marriage after a crippling accident, our ancestors picking cotton and churning butter to buy the family land my aunt and uncle still call home.

Family stories have a way of grounding us, reminding us where we come from and bolstering who we are. They conjure days that have long traveled past us, days that would have escaped us entirely had not the stories held them captive for us. To speak them is to remember, to travel shared roads back in time to a place that was somehow brighter, more innocent, more agreeable than the place we are today.

Supper

We cannot stay in these ephemeral places. Nostalgia beckons us to try, but we cannot dwell in the rosy places of yesteryear where our stories are privileged to live. The stories always meet their end, queuing the present moment to abruptly break into our enjoyment and claim us back to face the reality of today.

And here a confession is due: I hate this.

Days are growing darker and time continues its relentless march forward and I wish – how I wish! – things could stop. Rewind. That I could just. go. back.

But for this wishful thinking I must repent because it falls pitifully short of Christ's own perspective on the matter. He never seemed to wish He was anywhere other than exactly where He was. He lived with a settled peace about the time continuum and understood His human place within it: "I know where I came from, and where I am going."[1]

Jesus knew where He came from. He knew the grandest of stories, the days of parted seas and prophets and feasts. He knew the stories before the Fall when things were *really* good. He knew the stories of the heavenly places from whence He'd come. He knew all these things but did not long to dwell there.

---

[1] John 8:14

He understood that all He had experienced in His timeless past was intended to point forward, to where He was going, to the place He'd be preparing for His Bride. He saw in His stories something we often miss in our own: signposts pointing forward.

These same signposts can be found in our stories, too. If we heed their message, we will learn that the good ole days do not seek to turn our gaze behind us in the vain hope of reliving them, but rather to stir in our hearts a longing for good things, and point us forward to the real hope of living what's next.

If we could expand and sanctify our imaginations enough to envision how very good our future in Christ is, we'd feel foolish for succumbing to that backward pull of nostalgia and fruitless wishing to relive lost days. In reality, all that we love in the stories of yesteryear are mere shadows of the absolute Goodness that we can only find fulfilled in a future with Christ.

The Bible assures us with a forward-looking promise, teaching that the rich history of ritual and sacrifice, prayer and festival - all that imbued the Jewish culture with transcendent meaning – is a mere shadow of the *really real* to come:

Supper

"The law is only a shadow of the good things that are coming—not the realities themselves."[1]

"These are a shadow of the things that were to come; the reality, however, is found in Christ."[2]

Everything points to Christ, finds its redemption in Christ, is fulfilled in Christ. And perhaps this is why I love listening to my dad's stories the most. They are full of signposts pointing us forward, helping us see in colorful, subtle, and unconventional ways the absolute Goodness of the Father. My dad's stories invoke heroism and bravery, taking risk and receiving reward, embarking on adventure and seeking out justice, laughing and feasting and enjoying victories. These are all foretastes of Tomorrow, reminders of a redeemed moment in time that is still yet to come.

His stories from the past are really intimations of future hope, holding a promise and reminding those of us who know Jesus that the place where He said He was going is real. It is the place to which our stories point us – the glorious, incorruptible, complete reality to come:

And they all lived happily ever after.

---

[1] Hebrews 10:1 NIV
[2] Colossians 2:17 NIV

then...He gave thanks...

Matthew 26:27 gnt

SUPPER

In Gratitude

Writing has been a faithful companion on my storied pilgrimage toward Home. It has served as a healing balm over wounds and a fuel over principled fires.

Writing this book has proven to be unfinished art and insufficient worship; it is a humble offering I leave at the altar for Jesus. I am all too aware of its inadequacies but am so grateful for the opportunity to worship Him in this small way.

For the stories that shaped this book, I thank God for my extensive and treasured Family, who taught me the art of Christian living, surrounded me as songs of deliverance, and inspired me to look back, that we might come together on common ground to look forward.

I am thankful especially to Juan Carlos, who endeavors to love me as Christ loves the church, and to Isabelle and Julieana, who are the spiritual arrows with which God has graced us, pointing forward into the future.

And most of all, I am thankful to Jesus, who imbues the everyday with glimpses of heaven and brings divinity to every dinner table.

www.ingramcontent.com/pod-product-compliance
Lightning Source LLC
Chambersburg PA
CBHW022042200426
43209CB00072B/1924/J